Amazon FBA

The 2015 Definitive Guide to Becoming Rich from Selling Physical products on Amazon FBA

Table of Contents

Introduction

Chapter 1: Amazon is a Better Fit for Your Online Business

Chapter 2: Be Successful from Home Using Amazon Tools and Your Own Business Plan

Chapter 3: Choosing Your Product and Your Market

Chapter 4: Using Amazon for Your Products and Suppliers

Chapter 5: Branding Yourself and Your Business

Chapter 6: Inventory Control

Conclusion

Introduction

I want to thank and congratulate you for downloading the book, "Amazon FBA". 6 Months ago I was working long shifts as a baker at my local corner shop. I had worked there for years doing shifts that started at 2am in the morning. Over the last 6 months, I have built an Amazing Online FBA Business and I'm proud to say that now I have much more time for my family. I'm now turning over over $20,000 dollars of physical product per month on my online store. It has truly changed my life and I want to impart my knowledge so that others can learn from my experience that I've gained.

This book contains proven steps and strategies on how to become a truly successful person using the Amazon FBA program. With this book as your guide, becoming a successful entrepreneur from anywhere around the globe will not be an impossibility.

Here's an inescapable fact: Read this book with an open mind and a will to succeed. Period. If you do that, you will walk away with the knowledge and skill set you need to get you on the path of having your own business and rapidly finding financial freedom. This is not a get rich quick scheme, however it is a blueprint for how to fast track your success and get ahead of the curve that is the Amazon FBA program.

We hope that you continue to reread this book, as it contains so much knowledge that being able to absorb an apply it all in one reading will be hard. It should remain as a core resource on your bookshelf for years to come. We've conveniently grouped all of the fundamental "Tips" and "How To's" in this book in one spot, for easy reference. This will allow you to spend more time focusing on your business and monetize on your online skills that you have learned.

It's time for you to become an amazing entrepreneur using Amazon. Don't hesitate. The journey of success with Amazon FBA awaits and financial freedom is just around the corner!

Chapter 1: Amazon is a Better Fit for Your Online Business

With the trend of online shopping soaring, those who have a business plan and a will to become successful can open, operate, and own a business. Using Amazon to do so is one of the easiest ways of writing your own path to success. Many have done it, many are doing it, and many will come to find out they should have done it in the first place. Become an entrepreneur with just a few clicks of your mouse and your keyboard.

Why is Amazon's FBA program such a good option compared to traditional online businesses?

Amazon's FBA (Fulfillment by Amazon) program puts everything at your fingertips. You are able to sell the products that you want and they will ship it for you. They have one of the most advanced fulfillment programs available for those who want to become online entrepreneurs.

FBA works this way. First, your product will be stored in the Amazon facilities and they will handle your inventory for you. Gone are the days when you have an order and have to make a special trip to the post office just to get the item shipped. The specially trained Amazon staff will fulfill each order that comes in and tracks your inventory in your stead. Your packaging and shipping is placed in the hands of those trained individuals and you are free to continue with the business aspect of running your business. You will be able to reach a customer base that would otherwise be untouchable in normal circumstances. It has been reported that 71% of the FBA users have seen at least a 20% increase in their sales since they started using the program.

Amazon Prime

Everyone is familiar with the ever-so-convenient program that Amazon has to offered called, *"Amazon Prime"*. It offers free shipping on certain orders and even has other great features to offer. Your products can be included in this program to ensure a more enticing appeal to those shoppers just itching to hit the "Add To Cart" button. You are not charged for the Amazon Prime shipping options either, which is definitely a bonus for you and the Prime member.

Customer Service

Using Amazon provides other benefits that an average and large business owner can enjoy. Customer service can be such a hassle, right? If you have ever worked in retail or other public-oriented positions, then you are fully aware that there are times when no matter what you do, you simply cannot make certain people happy. Of course, there are also some situations wherein the customer is plainly just not happy with a product. Nonetheless, you no longer need to fear such cases as Amazon customer service specialists will handle your customer service for you. Those unhappy customers will soon be happy when they deal with the trained customer support staff of Amazon. You will not have to handle calls about products or returns, Amazon does that for you when you use the FBA program.

Amazon FBA Program Pricing

If you are worried about the price of the FBA program - stop. The FBA program is a "pay as you go" type of program. You will not have to pay an arm and leg to get started in this fantastic program. You are charged for the storage space that is used and the orders that Amazon fills. The cost of shipping the product is already included in the fees with no additional charge. For the Amazon Prime option, that is extended to the Prime members.

How to use Amazon's FBA Program to Run Your Business from Anywhere

Where there is Wi-Fi, there is a place to run your own business. It is extremely easy to use the FBA program. There are ultimately five steps to use this program and virtually run your business from anywhere on the globe. Think about sitting in a boat and fishing while your bank account is raking up the dollars. You can even be utilizing the time to build your business further. So, here are the steps:

Step 1: Send in your products to the trusted Amazon staff.

All you have to do in this step is to send in your used or new products to the Amazon Fulfillment centers. You will then upload the listings to the Amazon system, which will allow you to choose as many products as you prefer. Print the PDF product/shipment labels that are provided by Amazon. At this point, you will be able to use Amazon's discounted shipping or the carrier of your choice.

Step 2: Amazon then stores your products.

Once Amazon receives the shipments of products, they will catalog and store your products in the ready-to-ship inventory section. They will scan your product/inventory and record the item dimensions for storage and shipping purposes. You are able to track the entire inventory on its way in and out on the integrated online tracking system they provide.

Step 3: Products are ordered by customers.

Customers are always on the lookout for specific products and products that seem like a "must-have" and with your product already being available, you will receive orders quite quickly. They will order through the Amazon site or on another e-commerce channel that is set up through your own business website.

Your products, which are listed, are available for Amazon Prime members, but as such, they will not affect the price of your shipping. You will reach a global market instead of a specific target group that you have a hard time reaching. Amazon will also handle the conversion and international shipping for you.

Step 4: Inventory Control and Shipping Orders

Once an order comes in, the Amazon staff will fulfill the order and track the inventory. They will locate the products for each order using their web-to-warehouse picking and sorting system that is put in place for impeccable inventory control. Customers are able to combine the orders with other products to produce an easier ordering experience, which will keep the customer coming back for more.

Step 5: Your products are shipped and support is even provided.

The fulfillment centers ship your products to all of those who have ordered your items. They will pack the product and ship it. Amazon handles the shipping fees as your part is already taken care of in the FBA program fees. Each order includes a tracking number for the customer. Should the customer have any issues and concerns, the trained Amazon customer service providers will handle the situation for you.

Chapter 2: Be Successful from Home Using Amazon Tools and Your Own Business Plan

Making sure you have the time and money.

Of course, just as any business is, you will need to plan on spending time and money to start your Amazon business venture. You will need to factor in time for specific aspects of getting your online business booming. Here is a list that includes many aspects that will need to be factored into your schedule.

Product Preparation – You will need to collect the products that you will be selling using the FBA program. Whether it is used items or new items, you will need to pack it all together to send in to the fulfillment center. (This will cost a small amount due to packing materials and shipping your products to the fulfillment centers.)

Make a List – Make a list of the items that you are sending in as well as your pricing information. This list will make it much easier when you enter the information into the system for Amazon to sell in your behalf.

Trends – You will need to spend some time looking at trends to project your future sales properly. This will also help you anticipate re-ordering, making, as well as supplying more of your product to the fulfillment centers for customer orders.

Advancement of Knowledge - There are resources for the FBA members to utilize. There are seller stories to learn from, support personnel to ask questions, tutorials/training to advance further in your knowledge, as well as webinars for fresh ideas and tips that you may not know about.

Having the Right Mindset

It takes a special person to be able to hold a business together. This is definitely an easy way to get out there and get sales. However, it takes an appropriate mindset to start and succeed. There will be points in time when you may want to give up. Just remember, the rule of thumb for new business owners is that, money is not made in the first year of business due to putting money back into the business. Luckily for you, the FBA program takes the weight off of your shoulders by cutting those costs to a minimum so that you will obtain profit sooner than expected.

Successful people may be different from each other. Nevertheless, there are key aspects of their ways of thinking that helped make them and keep them successful. Here are the tips that you should follow to keep a successful mindset going.

Faith and Support

Just as other entrepreneurs, you will learn that there will be times that you will need to sacrifice. This is true in any and all industries when you are the "New Kid on the Block". You will be supplying the center with your products. This may mean that you will run low or even run out of products and will need to skip on that "out night" to obtain more items to send to the centers. This may seem like a negative situation, but this is definitely a good one. You want to sell out. This means customers love your products and the profits will be rolling in before you know it. It is important to have faith as well as support yourself morally in knowing what you want and going after it.

Expect Success

Entrepreneurs expect success. This is a good thing. Envision yourself as a successful person and you will be. This mindset adds in your drive to be successful. If you go into business with a low or negative (doubtful) mindset, then you will be setting yourself up for failure. You will not fight as hard, be as productive, or as creative. You need to prepare for the worst and expect the best when going into business. Never doubt yourself and strengthen your will to become successful. You will also become a magnet for those with the same mindset and network. This will be a good way to help your business grow.

Self-Confidence

Another aspect of having a winning entrepreneurial mindset is to have self-confidence. Self-confidence is the key in providing you with the ability to overcome any adversity. The entrepreneurial path is often full of good and bad experiences that you will find either rewarding or a little torturing. You will need to rely on your inner confidence and strength to keep yourself moving forward.

Healthy Self-Esteem

Entrepreneurs have a belief that achievement, accomplishments, and winning are parts of being successful and this is by far the truth. However, some of those who experience these do not own them. You will need to recognize all victories from small to large and own them proudly. These accomplishments are yours and you fought for them. Be proud! Allow your victories to fuel your next set of victories.

Positivity

Do not get positivity and self-confidence confused. Positivity represents your thoughts. In every situation there is a "silver lining". Although it may be hard to find at times, there is definitely one and you just have to find it. This way of thinking does get easier as time passes by.

With regards to positivity in the terms of beginning a business, you will need to realize that your products and services are worth every cent that they are listed for on Amazon. Watch the way you think on a normal basis. Thinking negatively will offer you negative outcomes. When you keep a positive outlook you will find that your outcomes will also be positive. Before you begin your work each day, remind yourself why you are doing it, remember small victories, envision your successful future, and then ask yourself if you are ready to succeed. This should be a good reminder as well as motivation to keep you going.

Having the Right Tools

Having the right tools is very important for the success of your business. You will always need to be prepared just like many other businesses, which have flourished. There are typical aspects of being prepared that will not need to be taken care of since Amazon FBA program takes a lot of your metaphorical plate. There are a few that you will still need to take care of on your end. Those would include the following:

Finance & Accounting: You will need to keep booking for your business. There are many software choices available that can be obtained for a small fee and at times even free.

Marketing: Although Amazon does take on many aspects of running your business for you, it is a great idea to come up with marketing ideas and strategies to really kick start your success.

Operations: If you plan on having more people involved other than yourself, you will need an operations plan. This operations plan will include how to contact each person, descriptions of the jobs per person, and other important information regarding how the business should be ran.

Website: This is a tool that some take for granted. A website is a great sales tool, business center, and idea generator while also helping the business to stay in contact with their customers. It is essential for success as of today due to the technical era we live in.

Inventory Control Software: This software will offer you trends and predict how many products you will have in demand next quarter. This is a great tool to stay ahead of demand and not miss out on potential customers and sales.

Chapter 3: Choosing Your Product

How to Choose a Product Niche

This is pretty easy. You will basically need to pick a niche that you are familiar with and even enjoy. If you have never gone fishing in your life, then you would not sell fishing poles. If you have never baked or consider yourself to be a bad baker, then you would not sell baking supplies. However, on the same note, if you are a great painter and love to use acrylics, then selling painting supplies would be great. You know the trade, you are aware of what products are needed to start painting, and so forth.

Find the Best Product to Sell

If you would like to be successful, then you will need to realize that it not only depends on customer service, but the sales also depend on the ability of the product to sell. This directly relates to the demand of the product. You will need to pick a profitable product. Fortunately, there are steps you can follow to find the perfect product.

Step 1: Finding a good product.

There are wholesale sites where you would be able to order products from for a minimal fee. You will be ordering in bundles, lots, or bulk. This will also cut down the initial cost of your product that you are selling. For instance, if you are selling specific horsehair paint brushes and receive a bulk shipment from a wholesaler your cost per brush will be low. Check out the math below:

(1 Bulk order of Paint Brushes (Quantity: 100) = $50.00)

This translates to $2.00 per brush. If you sell them for $5 apiece, this is lower than your competition (which draws in more sales), then when you sell the whole box of paint brushes, you will have sold all the brushes for $250.00. This means you have made a $200 profit.

There are people who order from other countries as well. China has been supplying many products for a very long time. Purchases made from China will take a long time to ship to you, yet they offer an even larger profit margin.

Tips for Good Products:

Light and small enough for easy packing and shipping. The bigger the product is, the more costly it will be for the customer in terms of shipping.

Specific Products (Niche) are best. It is best to stick to just one or two products. If you have too much of a variety then your sales will be less compared to just zoning in on one product. So, a couple of products would be best.

Keep the price bearable. It is a rule of thumb to only sell a product that costs anywhere from $10 up to $200. Although the price seems great to you, it does not seem feasible to your customer. You will obtain more sales if your pricing is modest. Stay away from expensive products.

Constant stream of customers. It is best to keep away from seasonal items. It will provide you with inconsistent sales and then you will fight for the same customers next season. This includes holiday items.

Keep your margins open. It is also a rule of thumb to mark your product up 100%. The markup is there to serve you not only with just profits, but also room for profit loss like broken products that were returned and as a sales tool for discounts and coupons. For example, if you purchased the paintbrush for around $2.00 per paint brush, then each brush should at least be marked up to $4.00 each.

Tips on Products to Stay Away From:

High quality standard mechanical items that offer warranties. This includes items such as power tools, machinery, as well as other items of this nature.

Items that are already sold by large retailers like Wal-Mart, K-Mart, Best Buy, or other competitive chains similar to these. If these giant retailers have them, then you will not have the sales that you will otherwise have with a deeper niche product.

Items that require special shipping instructions or fragile items. This is self-explanatory. Should the item break, then you will have to replace it and this will just turn into a nightmare and a possible profit loss.

Items that are sold by "Power Sellers". These items are products, which are already being sold by many people. Think about our local lovely Avon lady. There are already so many people selling this product that the market is so saturated that there is no money to be made. It is too divided.

Items that are trademarked. This will wind up in court. Keep your product legal and unique.

Step 2: Research Products

You can find trends on Amazon to see what areas of sales is trending and go from there. Research on products related to the niche you have figured out earlier. You can do it by category like Men's Clothing or Home Décor. You can look at the pricing of other sellers so you can learn more.

Step 3: Find and Test the Suppliers

You will need to do a little extra research in this step. You will do a search for suppliers of your product. A simple way to do this is to type your product type followed by the word "supplier" in the search bar of your favorite search engine.

Make a list of 3 to 10 different supplier contact emails. Then, produce a generic email that asks for additional information if it is not already listed on their websites. Compare your cost per unit and quality of the product, and then pick your supplier. To ensure that your name stays untarnished, make certain you sample the product before you purchase it for resale.

Chapter 4: Using Amazon for your products and suppliers.

How to Source Your Products & Your Suppliers

In order to really grasp the selling point of your product, you will need to know your product thoroughly - like the back of your hand. You will have had to use it, studied it, and liked it yourself. You have to believe in the product. Would you be able to sell a beverage that tasted like dirt? Probably not. You have to at least like the product you are offering to your customers.

How to Launch a Product on Amazon

There are steps for listing your product on Amazon. First, you will need to know what category your products or items go under. Here is a guide on where to place your product. This guide will show you the category name, the type of products that go in this category, the conditions of the product that is allowed, and if there needs to be approval for this product to be listed in this category.

Category: Amazon Device Accessories
Product Types: Amazon Device Accessories
Allowed Condition/s: New, Refurbished, Used
Approval Needed: No

Category: Amazon Kindle
Product Types: Amazon Kindle
Allowed Condition/s: Used

Approval Needed: No

Category: Baby (No Apparel)
Product Types: Nursery, Feeding, Gear
Allowed Condition/s: New
Approval Needed: No, Possible on Holidays

Category: Books
Product Types: Books, Calendars, Card Decks, Sheet Music, Magazines, Journals
Allowed Condition/s: New, Used
Approval Needed: No

Category: Camera Photo
Product Types: Cameras, Camcorders, Telescopes
Allowed Condition/s: New, Refurbished, Used
Approval Needed: No
Category: Cell Phones
Product Types: Phones
Allowed Condition/s: New, Refurbished, Used, Unlocked
Approval Needed: No (Must meet certain requirements)

Category: Consumer Electronics
Product Types: Televisions, CD Players, Car Audio, GPS
Allowed Condition/s: New, Refurbished, Used
Approval Needed: No (Maybe for certain products)

Category: Electronics Accessories
Product Types: Audio, Video, Camera, Photo, Cell Phone, Car Electronics, Computer Accessories, Office Accessories
Allowed Condition/s: New, Refurbished, Used
Approval Needed: No (Maybe for certain products)

Category: Home Garden
Product Types: Kitchen, Dining, Pet Supplies, Furniture, Décor, Bedding, Bath, Craft, Hobby, Home Appliances, Storage, Patio, Lawn, Garden, Pool Supplies, Landscaping, Snow Removal, Generators
Allowed Condition/s: New, Refurbished, Used, Collectible
Approval Needed: No

Category: Music
Product Types: CDs, Cassettes, Vinyl, Other Recordings
Allowed Condition/s: New, Refurbished, Used, Collectible
Approval Needed: No (Maybe for certain products)

Category: Musical Instruments
Product Types: Guitars, Orchestra, Recording Equipment
Allowed Condition/s: New, Refurbished, Used, Collectible
Approval Needed: No

Category: Office Products
Product Types: Supplies, Furniture, Printers, Calculators
Allowed Condition/s: New, Refurbished, Used, Collectible
Approval Needed: No

Category: Outdoors
Product Types: Outdoor Gear, Sports Apparel, Cycling, Action Sports
Allowed Condition/s: New, Refurbished, Used
Approval Needed: No

Category: Personal Computers
Product Types: Desktops, Laptops, Drives, Storage
Allowed Condition/s: New, Refurbished, Used
Approval Needed: No

Category: Software/Computer Games
Product Types: Business, Media Education, Utility, Security, Children's Software/PC Games
Allowed Condition/s: New, Used
Approval Needed: No (May for certain products.)

Category: Sports
Product Types: Exercise/Fitness, Hunting Accessories, Team Sports, Licensed/Fan Shop, Athletic Apparel, Boating/Fishing, Game Room,
Allowed Condition/s: New, Refurbished, Used, Collectible
Approval Needed: No

Category: Tools/Home Improvement
Product Types: Hand/Power Tools, Plumbing, Electrical, Building Materials, Appliance Parts
Allowed Condition/s: New, Refurbished, Used
Approval Needed: No

Category: Toys/Games
Product Types: Infant/Preschool, Learning/Exploration, Toys, Ride-Ons, Action Figures, Dolls, Board Games, Arts, Crafts, Hobbies, Furniture
Allowed Condition/s: New, Collectible
Approval Needed: No (Maybe for products during holidays)

Category: Video-Games, Video-Game Consoles
Product Types: Game Consoles, Consoles Games, Console Accessories
Allowed Condition/s: New, Used, Collectible
Approval Needed: No (Maybe for certain products)

Launching Your Product on Amazon

Although this step is easy, it does still take some time and attention to detail. Follow these instructions in order to list your product the right way and begin selling your inventory.

Step 1: Product Information

Each product will have its own product page where customers are able to learn about the product. It includes information like details about the product, reviews from customers who purchased your product, and more. This is specifically called the "Product Detail Page". Here is a breakdown of the information that is required for the page.

Title Requirements: Having the proper title for your product is the key to effectively sell it online. Customers will discover the product by its title. It should have a precise and short description. Do not include information like pricing or promotion information in the title. An example of a good title is, *"Horse Hair Paint Brush Fine"*.

Description/Bullet Points: This is where you will be using precise information to give the potential customer some information at a glance. Customers do not want to spend 15 minutes reading paragraphed information about a product, they may or may not purchase. Keep each feature of the product short and sweet when building your bullet list.

Image Requirements: Customers do not purchase products without knowing what it looks like first. It is imperative that you acquire some great quality images of the product that you are selling. Should the product open (like a storage container), get an image of it opened as well as closed.

The product should take approximately 80% of the image. For crisp and clear images, they should be at least 500x500 pixels. Although 1000x1000 is best for a better-detailed image.

Search Terms: There will be five fields in which key search terms will need to be entered. This will help customers find your product. Each of the fields can contain up to 50 characters (letters, spaces, and numbers). Separate the terms with spaces and not commas. It is a great idea to put the title, manufacturer, UPC, and even the merchant in the key search terms. Do not waste your space to repeat terms. Once the term is already in there you do not need to add it again in a new phrase.

Product Classification: In order to be successful on Amazon, you will need to ensure that your product is listed right. If a customer is looking for your product they will be looking in the category in which it belongs. If the product is not listed in the correct category the customer will not see it and you will lose that sale. Amazon offers two different tools to ensure that you list it in the right place. In the download section of the Seller Central Help area, the Browse Tree Guide will help you if you are unsure of the correct placement of your product.

Step 2: Listing Your Product on the Amazon Site

There are different options for you to list products. The option will depend on the quantity of products that you will list. Each option does offer the inventory tracking.

Add a Product Tool: This tool offers a way to list up to 50 products. If you are listing one or more products, then this option is the best way to go.

Inventory File: If you have decided to sell multiple products that are not cataloged on Amazon as of yet, then this option will correspond to the primary product category. You will need to download the Excel template from the Seller Central area.

Listing Loader: This option allows you to use a simple template for products that are already listed on Amazon. It will require UPC/EAN codes for you to create your listings. You can download an Excel sheet from the Seller Central area.

Amazon Seller Desktop: If you would like to work offline (which will offer you more freedom during your entrepreneurship endeavors) you can use the Amazon Seller Desktop to list your items. You will download and install this onto your computer. You are able to list your products using this program. It offers a wizard-like functions to aid you in creating and maintaining your listings.

Should you choose to use one of the Excel templates to list your products, then once you have created the inventory file, save the file as a tab delimited text file. (This is found under Save As > File menu > Choose Test.)

It is recommended to first upload no more than twenty products at one time. This will allow you to get every detail right with minimal effort. Typically the listing will be updated within minutes. However, it is best to wait 24 hours for your products to appear on Amazon.

Step 3: Entering Your Account Settings

This is an important step that cannot be skipped. Listed here are all of the information that you will need to enter as well as a guide to help you enter the correct information for you to conduct business.

Confirm Business Name: When you go through the registration process, you will need to have a business name. This name will be displayed on Amazon, along with your legal name and business address. If your business is already registered, then you will need to enter the name exactly as it appears in the registration that was completed prior to Amazon. You are able to change this later should any information be incorrect or changed by simply going to "Settings" in the "Seller Central" area.

Contact Information for Customers and Amazon: You will need to supply an operating email that you are able to respond to for your customers and Amazon staff.

Shipping: You will need to set the location where your products will be shipping from. If you are part of the FBA program, then this will be from the fulfillment centers.

Payment Information: In order to set up the payments account, you will be required to provide Amazon a valid United States bank account. You will receive funds from the sales 14 days after the transaction is completed. This will be sent directly into your bank account.

Shipping Costs: This is included in the fees for the FBA program.

Shipping Service Levels and Regions: This will also be taken care of for those who are involved in the FBA program.

Step 4: Seller Profile

This is another important aspect of your business. This is the information that each customer will see when he or she is scanning the products that you have for sale. It is important to treat your name like your credit score. Should you receive any negative feedback, your seller profile will show this and future potential customers will be less likely to purchase products from you.

About the Seller: This is an important part of the information that you need to offer your customers. It needs to include when you started your business, your mission statement, if you have a brick and mortar location, and other information pertaining to your business. Your mission statement should be one sentence that sums up what you would like to do as a company. For example, if you have a business that offers artist supplies, your mission statement could be, "Our company strives to bring the highest quality of supplies for the highest of art made by you."

Logo: Every company should have a logo. Typically a company will use a specific font for their company name and it will be consistent throughout the entire branding process. Some companies also offer a simple shape or picture that is included with the company name. These attributes are put together as one picture or image that is put on products and associating websites and pages.

Refunds and Returns: This is vital. You will need to come up with guidelines regarding refunds and returns. If you are a part of the FBA program, then the Amazon staff will take care of these issues for your business.

Step 5: Tips and Advice for Selling

Here you will find many tips and advice on selling online with Amazon. It is important to read this and take as much from it as possible to become successful in running your own online business.

Check Orders Daily: Although you are enrolled in the FBA program, it is important to check your orders daily. This will help you track trends and stay on top of your inventory. If you are not checking daily, then you are risking your business as you might run out of products at the fulfillment center. If that happens, you will have nothing to offer to your customers and this is just bad business.

Inventory Control: You will need to watch your inventory to ensure that you stay fully stocked at the fulfillment centers. If you do not have the product the customer wants, then the customer may leave a negative feedback that will tarnish your seller reputation.

Pricing Accuracy: It is important to keep your products priced at fair and reasonable prices. If there are other products that are like yours, then it is a good rule to keep the price the same as theirs or lower. If you price the item higher than other similar products, then you will not sell that product well.

Be Accessible: You will need to ensure that you respond to your customers quickly with answers to questions that they send to you. If you do not respond they will move on to a seller that offers the same product, yet is more accessible to answer the questions they need answered.

Build Some Good Feedback: Customers pay attention to the ratings of the sellers before purchasing their order. If you have a negative reputation they will not purchase your product out of fear of poor quality, bad business practices, and more. Take care of your rating and your sales will just increase.

Find Answers: Take the time to look through and read any materials in the "Seller Central" area. It will help you conduct your business like a pro.

Common Terms to Familiarize Yourself With

Amazon Marketplace: This is a term that is used to describe the area in which the customer is able to shop from.

Amazon Standard Item Number (ASIN): This is a 10-digit item identifier placed on each product. Each of the ASINs is different, even when offering a SKU.

European Article Number (EAN): This is equivalent to the UPC that is used outside of the U.S. The EAN is a number, which encompasses 12 to 13 digits and is considered to be a product identification code.

Inventory: This is the list of all of the products that you have for sale.

ISBN: This stands for International Standard Book Number and is a 10-digit number that is unique to each published book.

Offer: This is an individualized listing of a product that will have a price listed, along with the quantity that is in stock and condition.

OLP – Offer Listing Page: This page has all of the offers for a particular product and lists all merchants that have it listed. A customer reaches this by using the search feature on the "Amazon Marketplace" page.

Product Detail Page: This is the page that the customer can utilize in order to see all the details about the product you have listed.

Universal Product Code (UPC): This is a primary identifier used in the U.S. for products other than published books. It is typically 12 digits long.

Chapter 5: Branding Yourself and Your Business

How to Grow Your Business

There are reasons why some businesses fail and some succeed. As covered earlier in the book, a negative mindset is definitely of the causes for failing. On this chapter, you will be able to read tips on how to obtain extra knowledge to ensure that your business is a success and that you do not sit on the sidelines while others collect what should have been your profit.

Do NOT simply meet the requirements or under deliver. You need to exceed the expectations of your customers. Not only will they become your loyal customers, but they will also send in more business your way. We are in the age of technology, but do not write off the power of "word of mouth".

Ask for feedback. It is not in bad taste to ask for a review of your product or service. Be simple about it by sending a "Thank You" card with the product and ask that they rate their experience and transaction. This will help you build a good reputation as a seller on Amazon.

Refer Customers: Should you receive a question about a product that you do not carry, do not be selfish. If you know of a seller who has that product, then by all means, refer the customer. However, make sure that you trust that customer and that you are not simply referring a name on the list. By doing this kind deed, this customer will keep you in mind when they do need a product that you offer.

Be Great: Offer exceptional experiences to each and every customer. This will keep them coming back to you for the product you offer and other products that you will be offering in the future. Offer kindness, understanding, and professionalism with each and every transaction, phone call, or email.

How to Brand Your Business

Whether the business is small, medium, or large, branding is extremely detrimental for the business to thrive and prosper. You will need to ensure that you have an effective branding strategy. Here is a guide to help you through in branding your new online business.

Brand Equity and Strategy

The branding strategy involves what, how, where, to whom, and where you plan on delivering your branding messages. Where will you advertise your business and products? The distribution channels are also a part of the strategic plan, as well as what you will offer verbally and visually as far as your brand is concerned.

You need to be consistent in your branding so that it leads to a strong equity. This means, it is adding value to your company and products. In the long run, this will ultimately help you when you are increasing your prices in the future. Take the classic branding experiences of the company Coca-Cola versus that of a generic soda company. Although they are selling the same product, Coca-Cola is known on a higher level than any other lower branded soda company. This is due to the mass branding that the company has conducted over the years.

Defining Your Specific Brand

You will need to define your brand. It is like taking a journey of self-discovery with your business. It may be difficult and time consuming at first, but the un-comfortableness is nothing in comparison to the finished product that sits in front of you waiting for your direction. Here are some questions to ask yourself to help you form your brand.

What is the mission statement of your company?

What are the benefits of using your products?

What are the features that your product has to offer?

What do the customers think of your company?

What qualities would you like to have associated with your company?

To aid you, you will need to build a guide to work from as you are setting up your company/seller profile for Amazon and for your own business website. This guide will make every step of the way easier. You will have all the information that you will need right in front of you on one page. You are able to use any text program that allows you to insert images (for logo).

Logo: Although this can wait until the other information is set forth, it is important to have your logo ready when building your seller profile and your business website.

Brand Messaging: What is the key message that you would like to communicate to your customers about your business? Every person working with your company should be made aware of the branding message.

Integrate the Brand: Your branding will extend to every aspect of your company. It will determine how you answer your phone line, what you say to your customers, the signature on your emails, and every other aspect of running your business.

Create Your Business "Voice": The voice of your company will be applied to any communication that is put into all materials that is visual. Ensure that it is conversational and friendly. Be professional and formal.

Tag Line: You will need to write a memorable and concise statement that encompasses the essence of the brand. It is much like the mission statement, but a little shorter.

Create Templates: Use the same color scheme for all of your documents, logo placement, and feel of the documents whether it is an invoice, statement, receipt, or other. It does not need to be fancy - just consistent.

Be Loyal to Your Brand: You will need to be loyal to your brand. This means you will need to follow your mission statement with each and every transaction. Customers will not return or refer others to you if you do not.

Consistency: This involves all of the above. You will need to have consistency through all aspects of your business. If you are inconsistent even once it could hurt your business. Always operate with a positive mind and with the well being of your business in mind.

Chapter 6: Inventory Control

Without inventory, you have no business. Staying ahead of the game is very important when operating your business. It is never a good idea to allow you to run low or out of the product that is in demand. Here you will learn how to project your inventory needs and allow yourself room to breathe.

Lead Time

When you have an order ready to be placed with your supplier, it will take a bit of time to reach the fulfillment center. This time is referred to as "lead time". If you are ordering from overseas, then the lead-time will be that of at least one month, at times it could take 2 to 3 months to be delivered to the recipient. There are many happenings that can take place during this time. For example, if you have an item that sells high during the holidays, then ordering extra a couple months prior to the season is a great idea to allow your inventory to stay stocked. The extra inventory that you order for this time period is referred to as "**safety stock**".

Formula to follow for reordering is:

safety stock + lead time demand = reorder point

Lead time demand refers to the demand of your product during the reordering process. How much do you anticipate on selling before you receive your next inventory?

Lead time (daily) x forecasted sales daily = lead time demand

Reorder Point

In order to calculate the reorder point, you will need to know the forecasted unit sales daily. You will need to factor in holiday seasons or other seasons that may play a factor. For example, if you are selling snowshoes your sales will be drastically higher during the winter months. You will also need to order a safety stock (extra inventory to ensure that you do not run out of product).

Lead time demand x 50% = safety stock

Going through these steps will ensure that your inventory never runs out. You will need to play with the numbers at times. As long as you do not run out of your inventory, then you will be safe. You will start to notice sales trends and will be able to anticipate the inventory needs with more precision as time passes. Ensure that you do have safety stock on hand to send to the fulfillment centers.

Conclusion

That's all folks!

Thank you again for downloading this book!

I hope this book was able to help you to understand where to start with your new business and how to operate your business for full success.

The next step is to outline your business plan and start selling your amazing niche product using the FBA program made available by Amazon.

Finally, if you enjoyed this book, please take the time to share your thoughts and post a review on Amazon. It'd be greatly appreciated!

Thank you and good luck!

Made in the USA
San Bernardino, CA
02 September 2015